INTERIOR PLANTING DESIGN FILE

INTERIOR PLANTING DESIGN FILE

Susan Van Gieson and Regina Kurtz

VNR VAN NOSTRAND REINHOLD COMPANY

Copyright © 1980 by Upper Level Graphics
Library of Congress Catalog Card Number 80-70578
ISBN 0-442-22344-7

Printed in the United States of America

Van Nostrand Reinhold Company Inc.
135 West 50th Street
New York, New York 10020

Van Nostrand Reinhold Company Limited
Molly Millars Lane
Wokingham, Berkshire RG11 2PY, England

Van Nostrand Reinhold
480 La Trobe Street
Melbourne, Victoria 3000, Australia

Macmillan of Canada
Division of Gage Publishing Limited
164 Commander Boulevard
Agincourt, Ontario M1S 3C7, Canada

16 15 14 13 12 11 10 9 8 7 6 5 4 3 2

Library of Congress Cataloging in Publication Data

Van Gieson, Susan.
   Interior planting design file.

   Includes index.
   1. House plants in interior decoration—Pictorial
works.   2. Foliage plants—Pictorial works.   I. Kurtz,
Regina.   II. Title.
SB419.25.V36   1984   747'.98   80-70578
ISBN 0-442-22344-7 (pbk.)

CONTENTS

INTERIOR PLANTING DESIGN FILE

INTRODUCTION

In recent years, plants have become an essential design element. They are used to organize space and complement the geometry of today's architecture. For the architects, interior designers, interior plant-scape specialists, and landscape architects this means that interior foliage plants are now an integral part of the design process. With this development in mind, *INTERIOR PLANTING DESIGN FILE* has been created as an aid to the design professionals who frequently require high quality, reproducible interior planting drawings in their work.

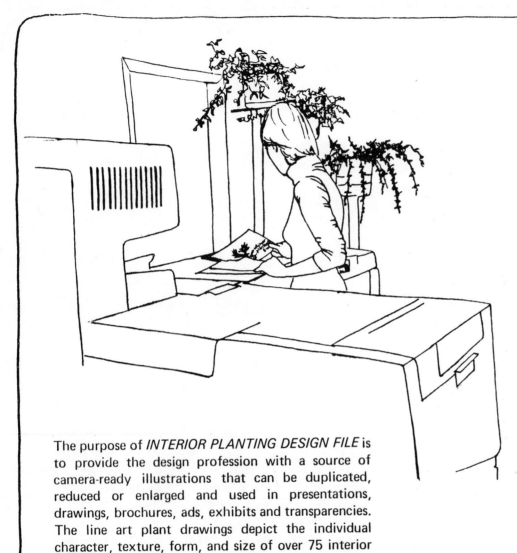

INTERIOR PLANTING DESIGN FILE is intended to not only save drawing time but to serve as a quick and easy reference of the physical differences between various interior foliage plants. Having all the plants drawn at the same scale provides the kind of information that can take hours to locate.

Our hope for this first edition is that it will be a useful tool for design professionals. We welcome suggestions and comments for the development of future editions.

The purpose of INTERIOR PLANTING DESIGN FILE is to provide the design profession with a source of camera-ready illustrations that can be duplicated, reduced or enlarged and used in presentations, drawings, brochures, ads, exhibits and transparencies. The line art plant drawings depict the individual character, texture, form, and size of over 75 interior foliage plant varieties. To increase their effective use, the plant drawings are presented in chapter 1 as individual studies, in chapter 2 at the same scale, and in chapter 3, selected plants are offered in groupings and as art studies.

INTERIOR
FOLIAGE PLANTS

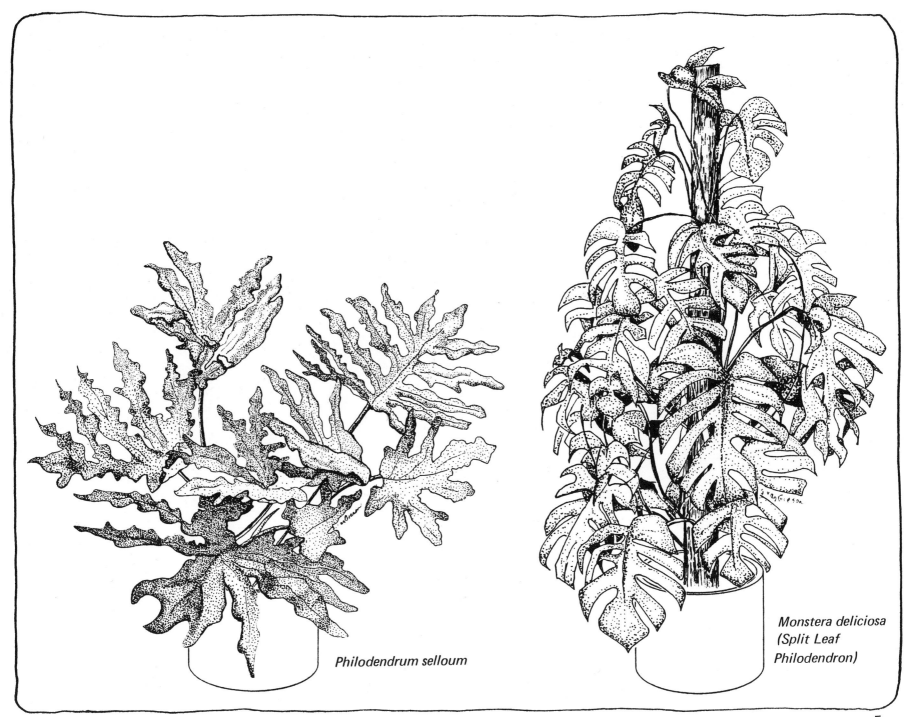

Philodendrum selloum

*Monstera deliciosa
(Split Leaf
Philodendron)*

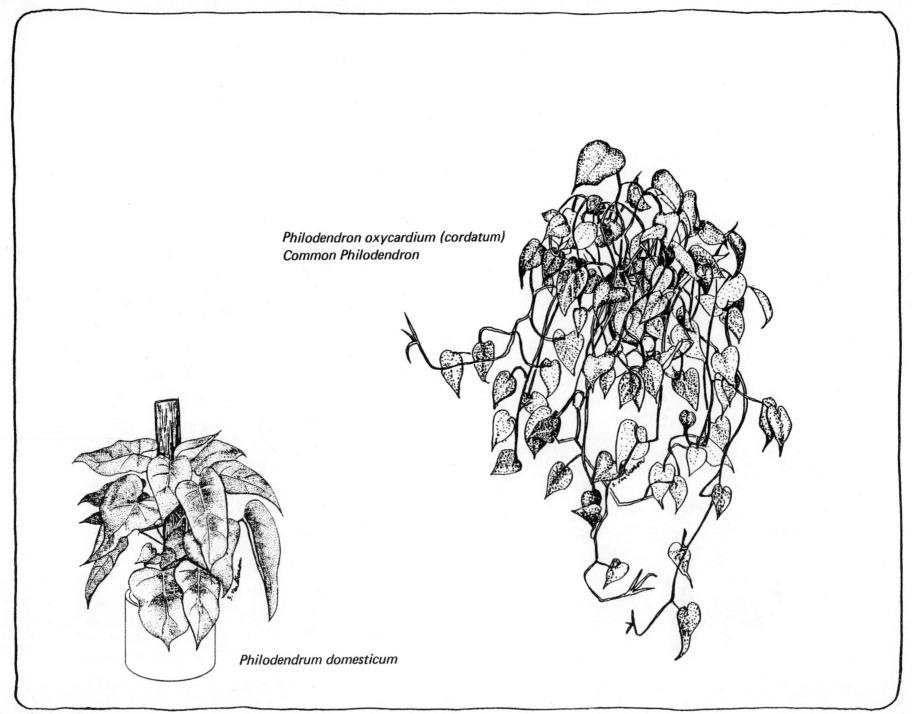

Philodendron oxycardium (cordatum)
Common Philodendron

Philodendrum domesticum

Ficus lyrata (Fiddle-Leaf Fig)

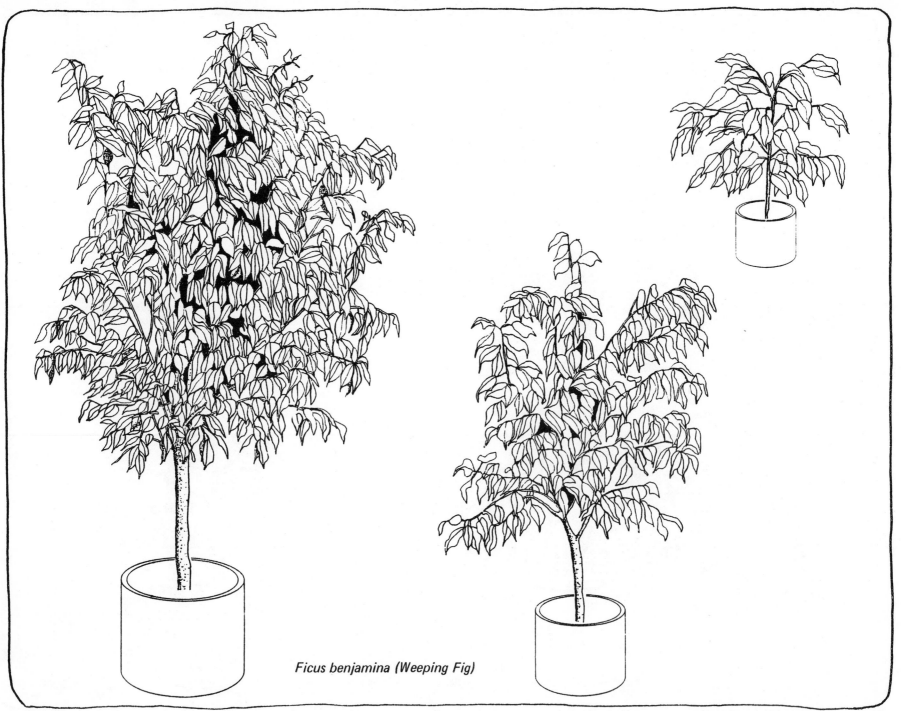

Ficus benjamina (Weeping Fig)

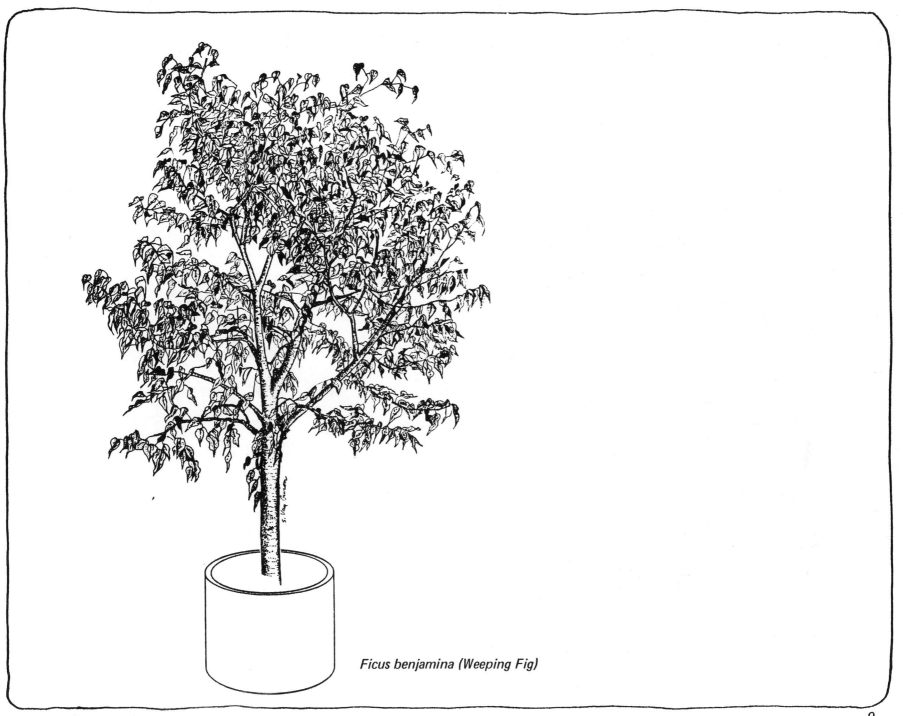

Ficus benjamina (Weeping Fig)

Ficus elastica (Rubber Plant)

Schefflera actinophylla (Umbrella Tree)

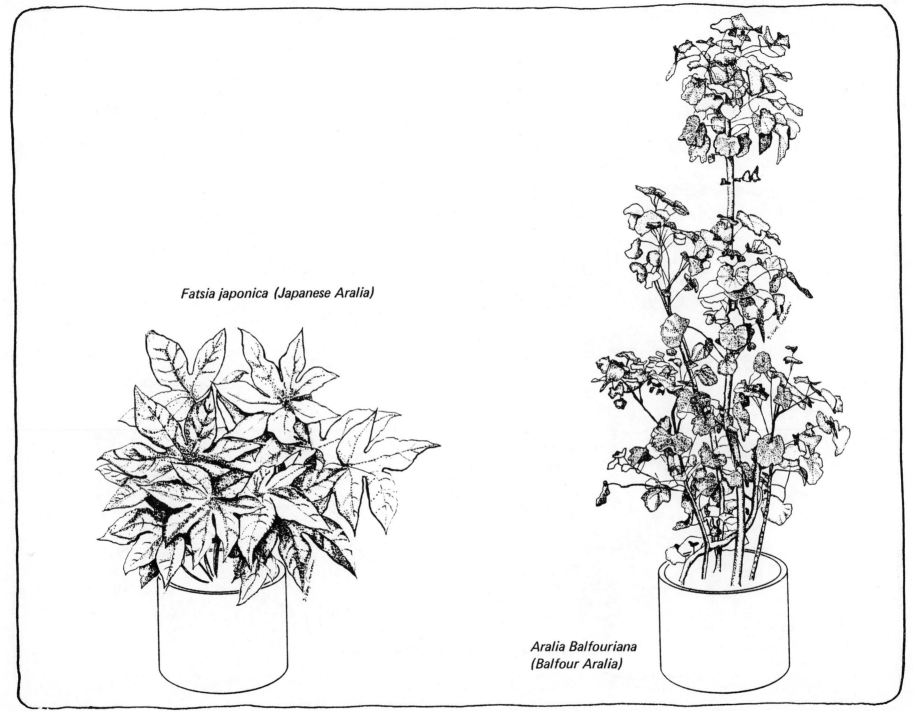

Fatsia japonica (Japanese Aralia)

*Aralia Balfouriana
(Balfour Aralia)*

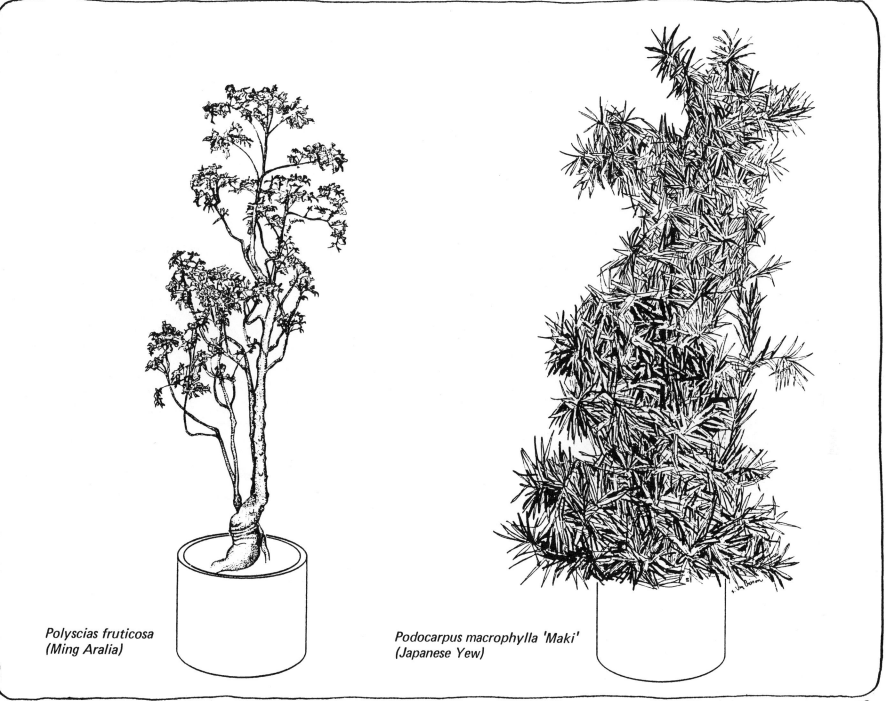

Polyscias fruticosa
(Ming Aralia)

Podocarpus macrophylla 'Maki'
(Japanese Yew)

13

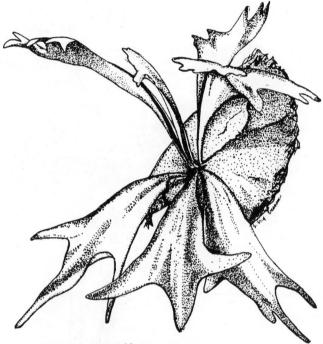

Platycerium bifurcatum
(Staghorn Fern)

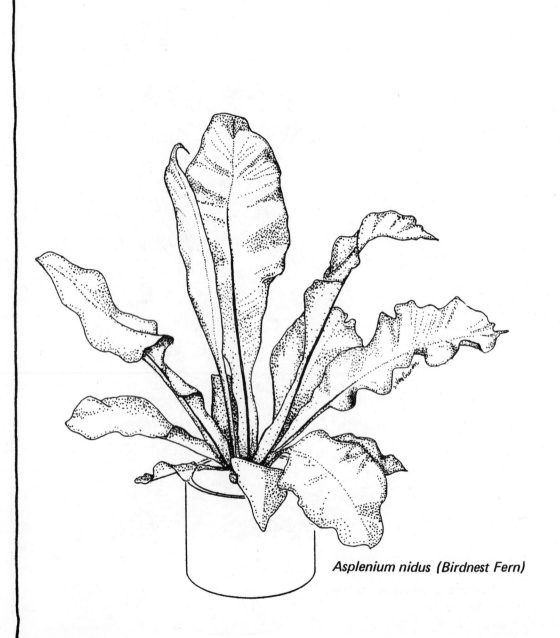

Asplenium nidus (Birdnest Fern)

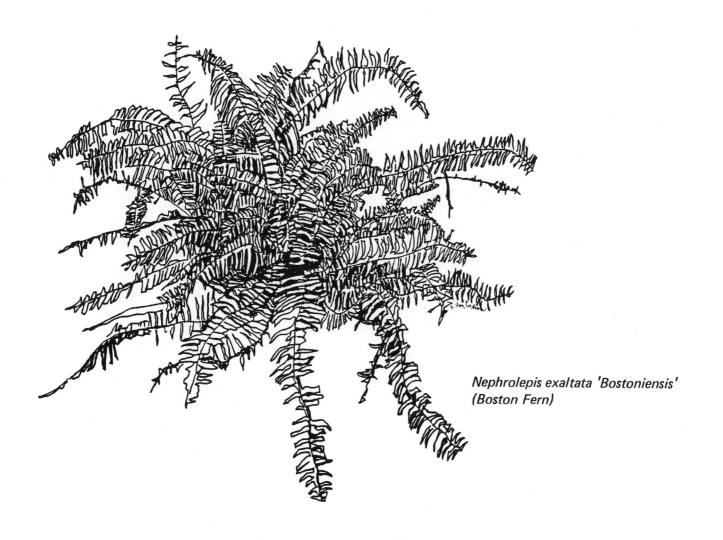

Nephrolepis exaltata 'Bostoniensis'
(Boston Fern)

Asparagus sprengeri (Asparagus Fern)

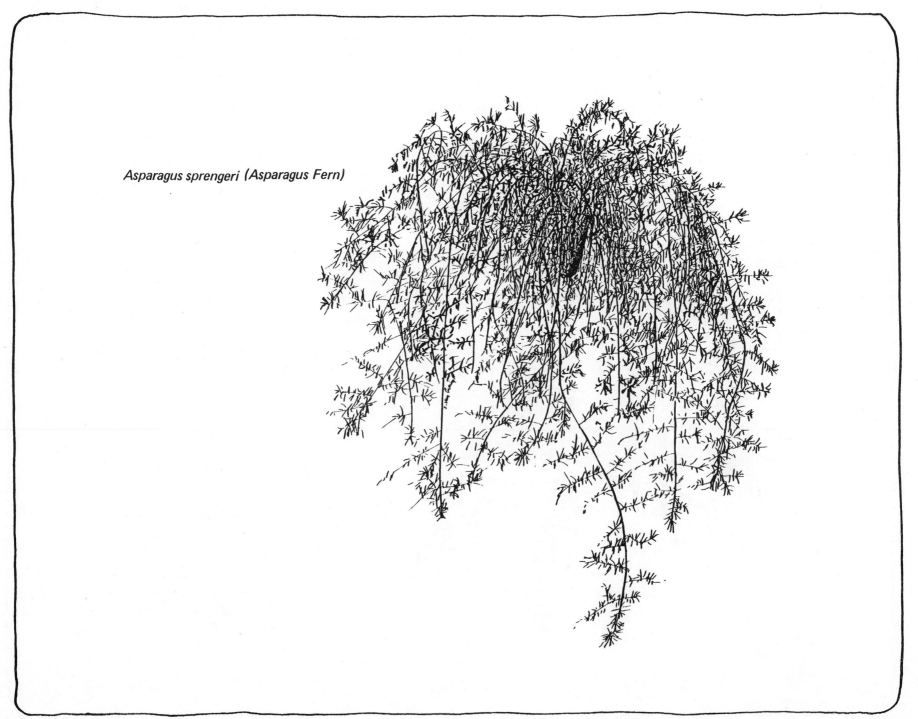

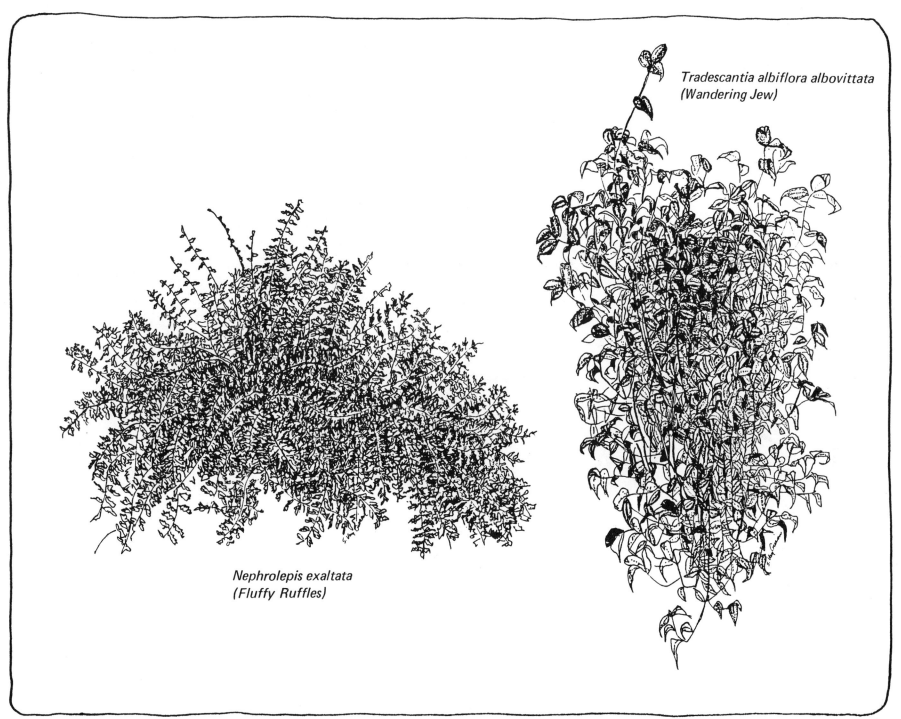

Tradescantia albiflora albovittata
(Wandering Jew)

Nephrolepis exaltata
(Fluffy Ruffles)

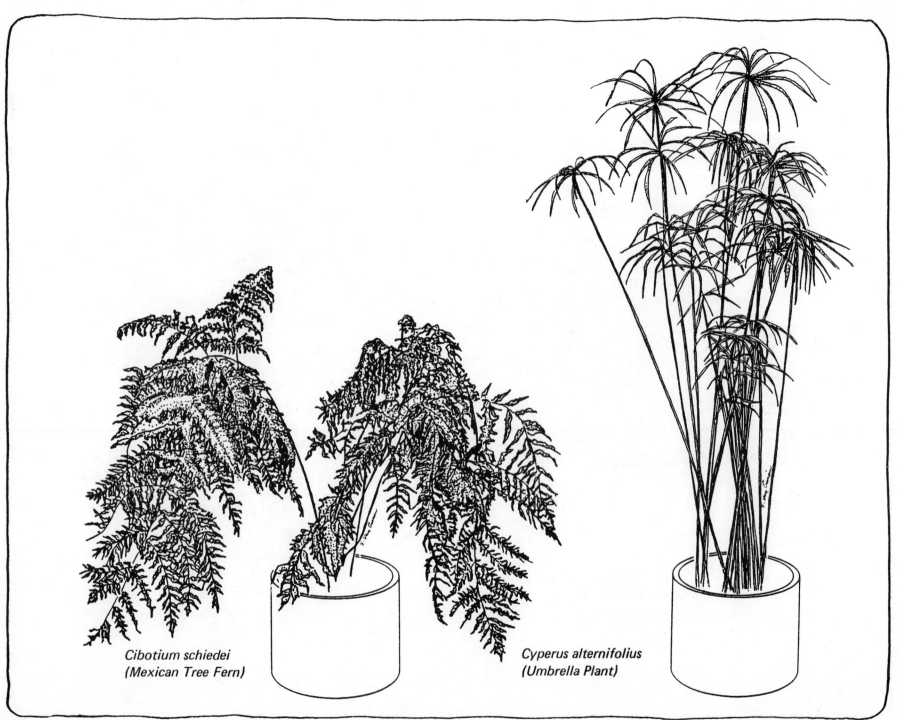

Cibotium schiedei
(Mexican Tree Fern)

Cyperus alternifolius
(Umbrella Plant)

Chamaedorea erumpens
(Bamboo Palm)

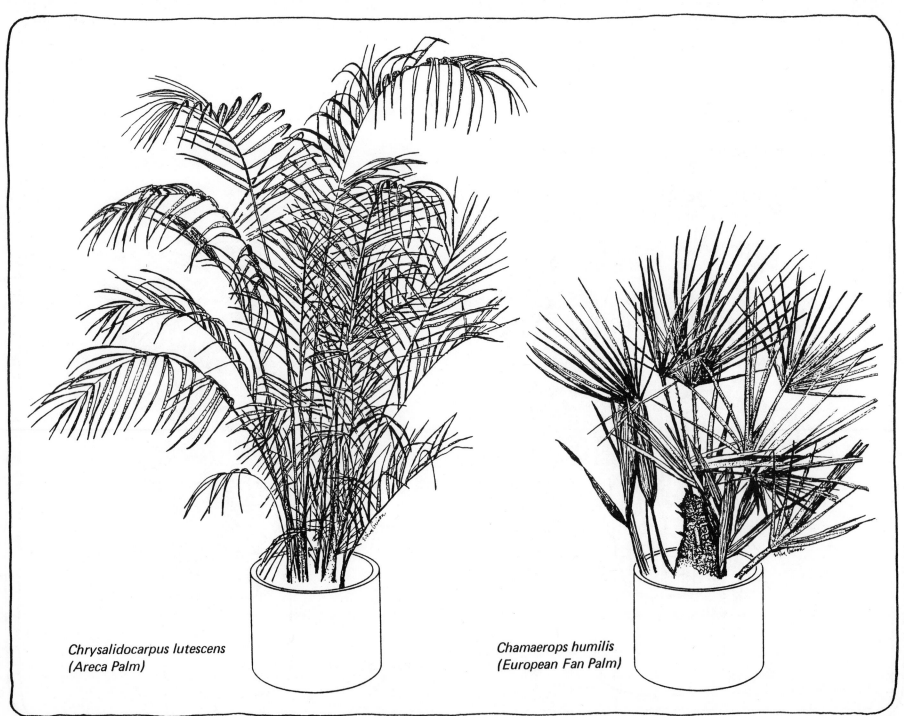

Chrysalidocarpus lutescens
(Areca Palm)

Chamaerops humilis
(European Fan Palm)

Phoenix roebelenii (Date Palm)

Howea forsteriana (Kentia Palm)

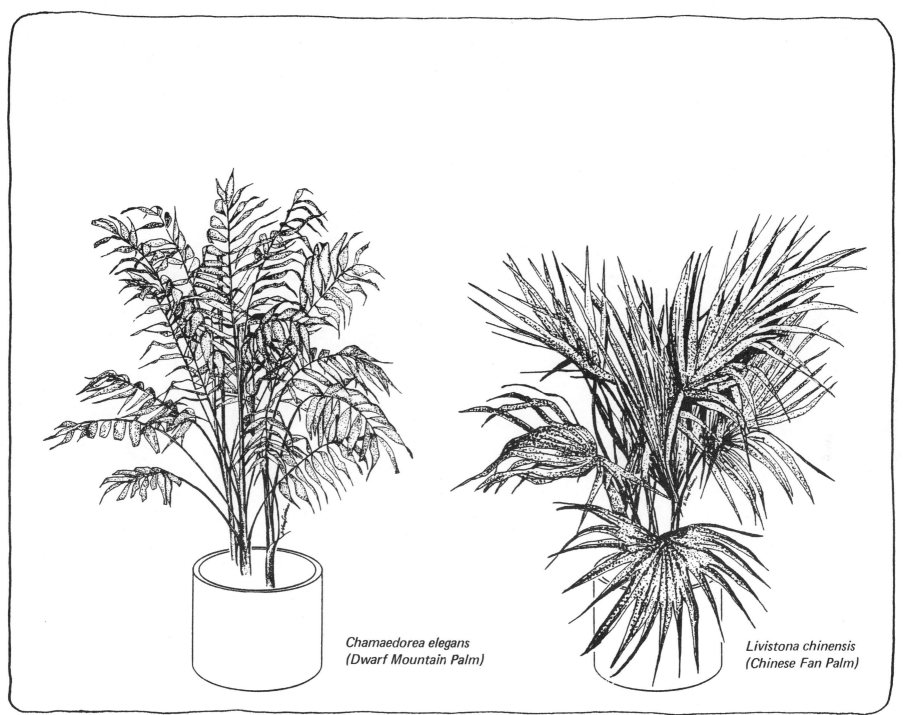

Chamaedorea elegans
(Dwarf Mountain Palm)

Livistona chinensis
(Chinese Fan Palm)

Rhapis excelsa (Lady Palm)

Dizygotheca elegantissima
(False Aralia)

Cycas revoluta
(Sago Palm)

25

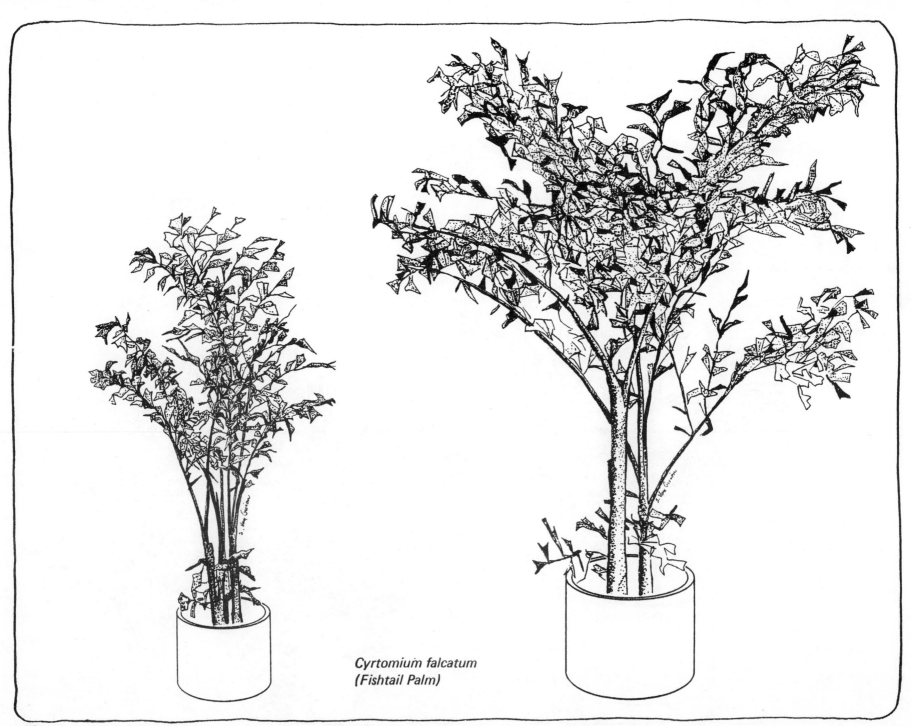

Cyrtomium falcatum
(Fishtail Palm)

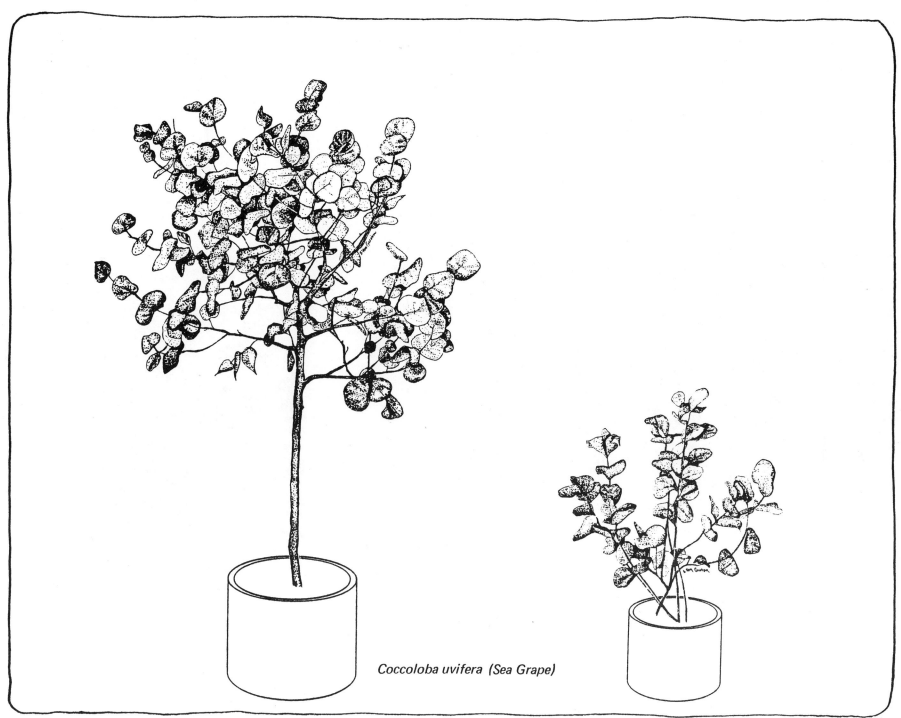

Coccoloba uvifera (Sea Grape)

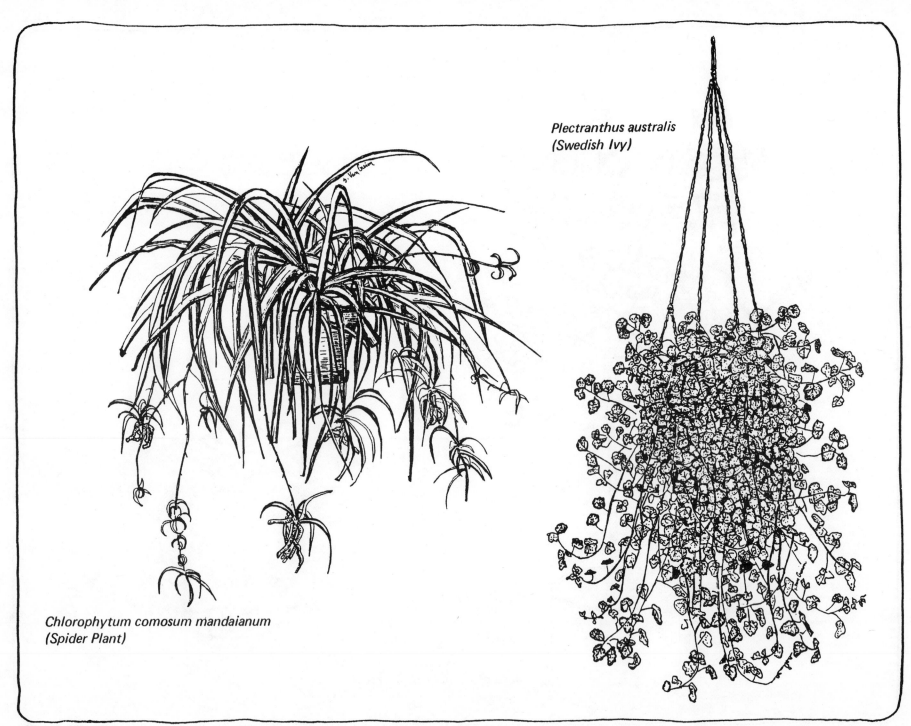

Plectranthus australis
(Swedish Ivy)

Chlorophytum comosum mandaianum
(Spider Plant)

Beaucarnea recurvata
(Pony Tail)

29

Hedera helix
(English Ivy)

Crassula argentea
(Jade Plant)

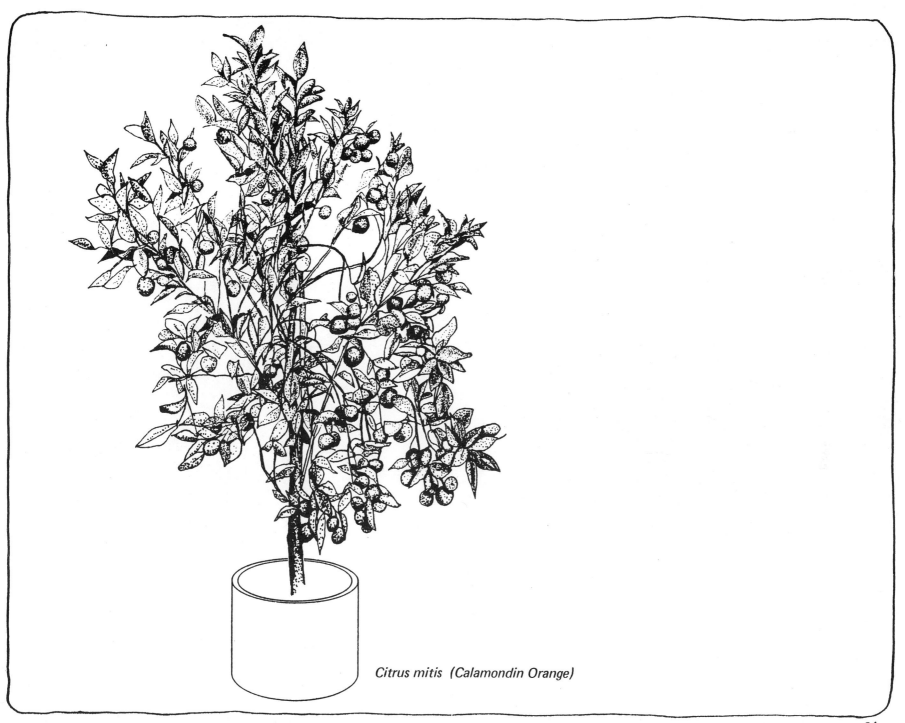

Citrus mitis (Calamondin Orange)

Pandanus veitchii (Screw-Pine)

*Pandanus veitchii
(Variegated Screw-Pine)*

Pleomele relexa
(Maylasian Dracaena)

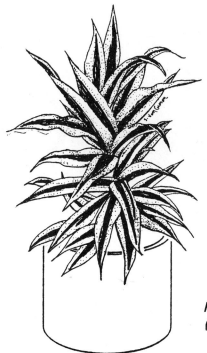

Pleomele reflexa
('Song of India')

33

Aechmea fasciata
(Bromeliad)

Sansevieria trifasciata
(Snake Plant)

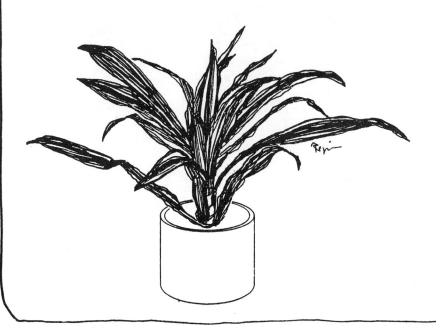

Dracaena deremensis 'Warneckei'
(Striped Dracaena)

Cissus antarctica
(Kangaroo Vine)

Dracaena deremensis 'Warneckei'
(Striped Dracaena)

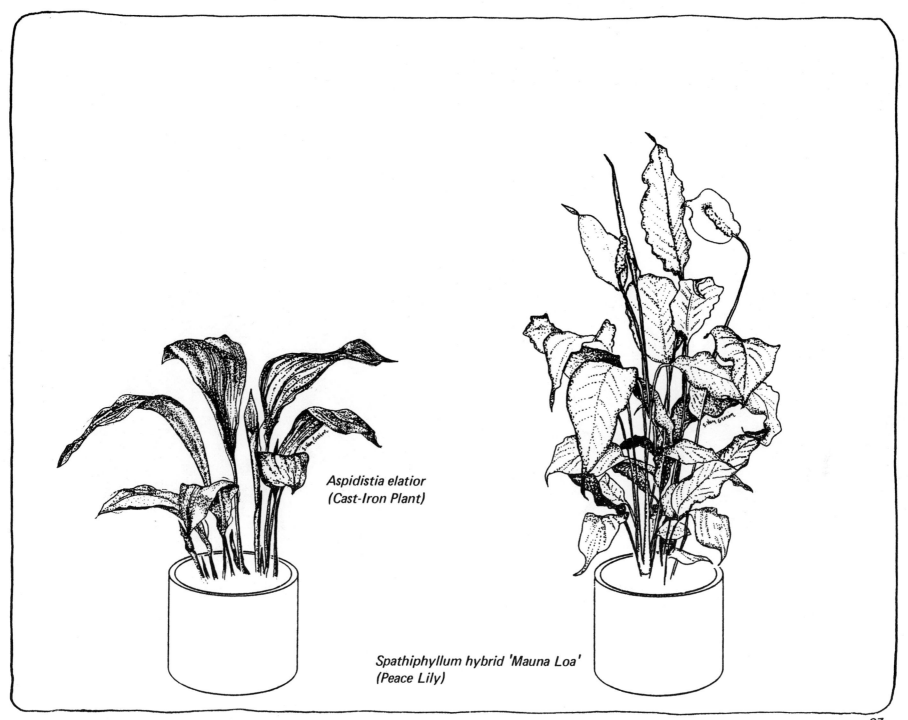

Aspidistia elatior
(Cast-Iron Plant)

Spathiphyllum hybrid 'Mauna Loa'
(Peace Lily)

Dracaena deremensis 'Janet Craig'
(Green Dracena)

Dracaena fragrans massangeana
(Corn Plant)

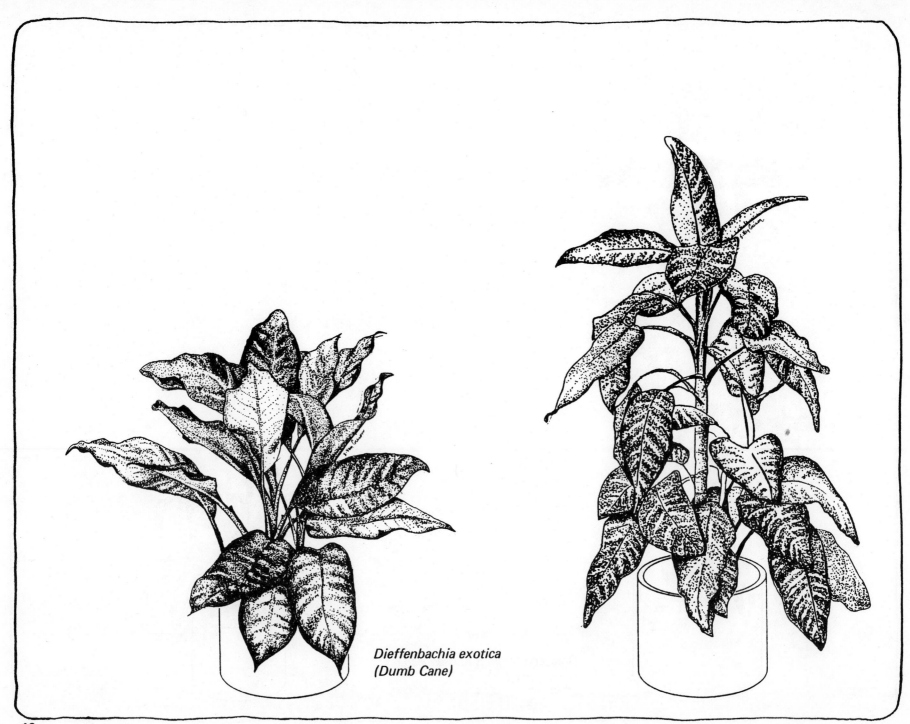

Dieffenbachia exotica
(Dumb Cane)

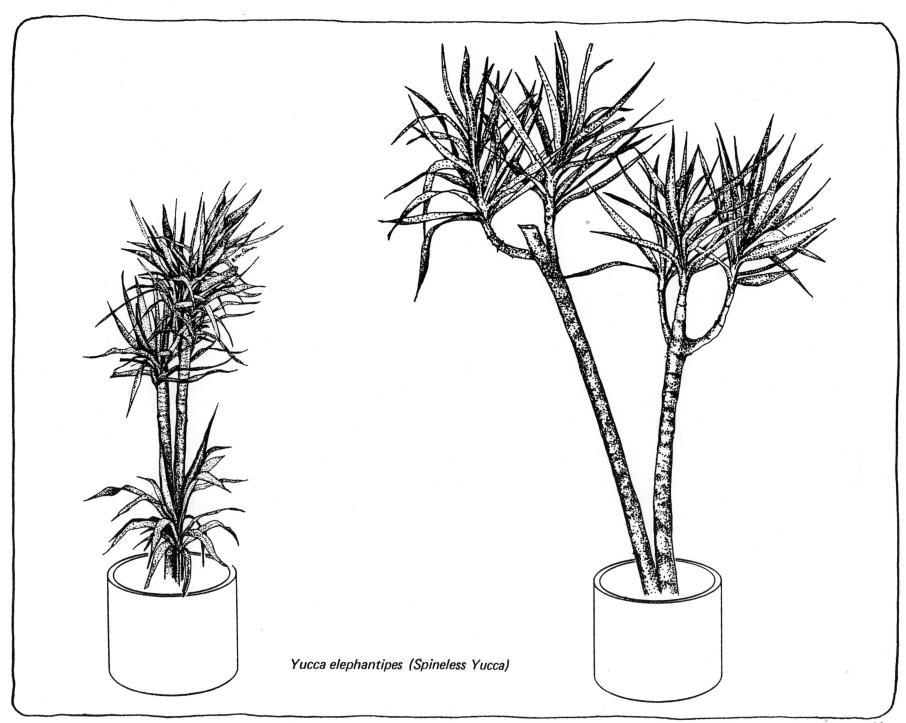

Yucca elephantipes (Spineless Yucca)

Dracaena marginata
(Madagascar Dragon Tree)

Euphorbia pulcherrima
(Poinsettia)

Araucaria heterophylla
(Norfolk Island Pine)

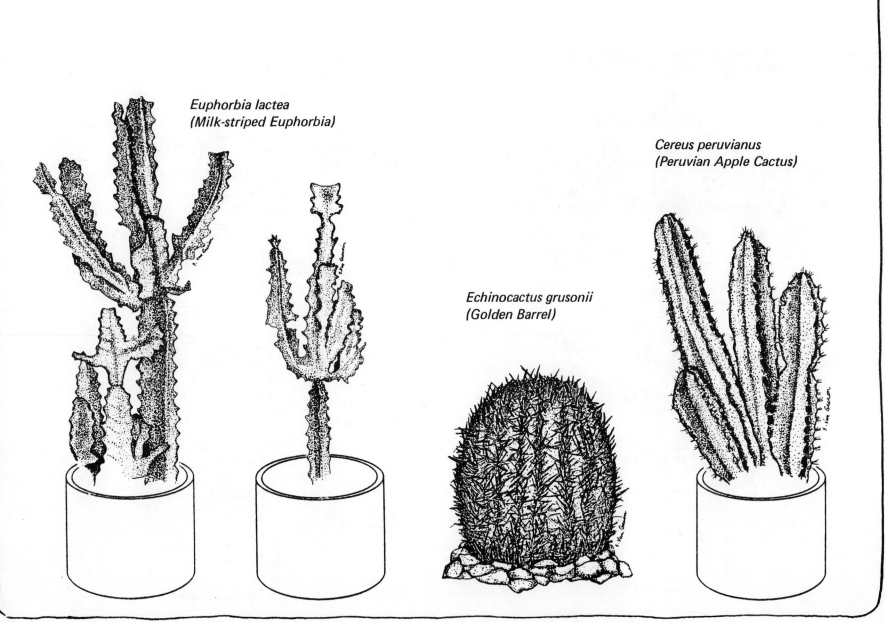

Euphorbia lactea
(Milk-striped Euphorbia)

Cereus peruvianus
(Peruvian Apple Cactus)

Echinocactus grusonii
(Golden Barrel)

44

INTERIOR
FOLIAGE PLANTS
TO SCALE

3/4" = 1'

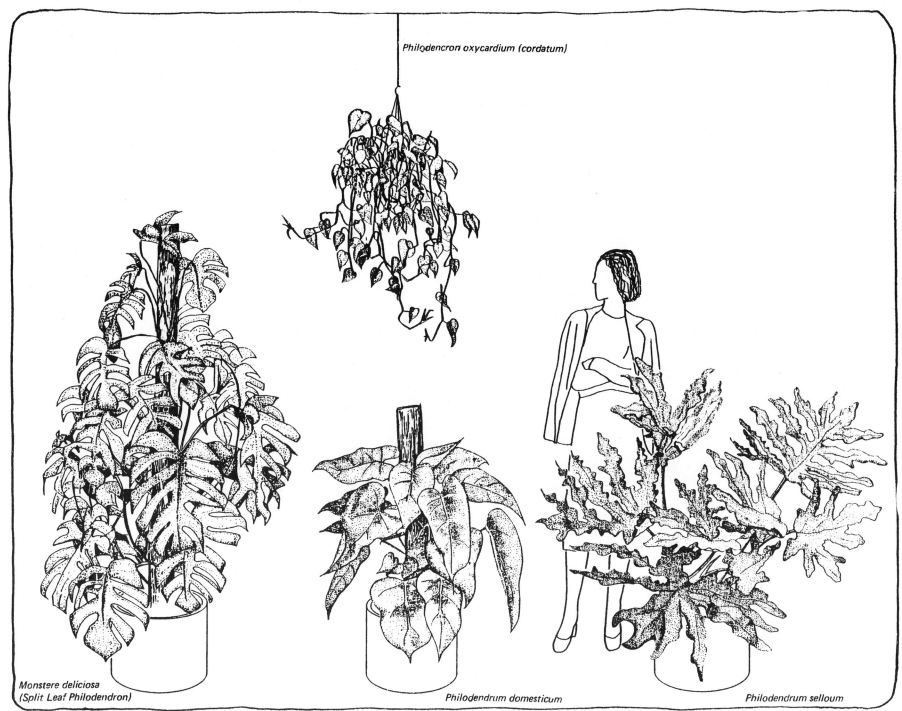

Philodencron oxycardium (cordatum)

Monstere deliciosa
(Split Leaf Philodendron)

Philodendrum domesticum

Philodendrum selloum

45

Cissus antarctica
(Kangaroo Vine)

Chrysalidocarpus lutescens
(Areca Palm)

. Howea forsteriana
(Kentia Palm)

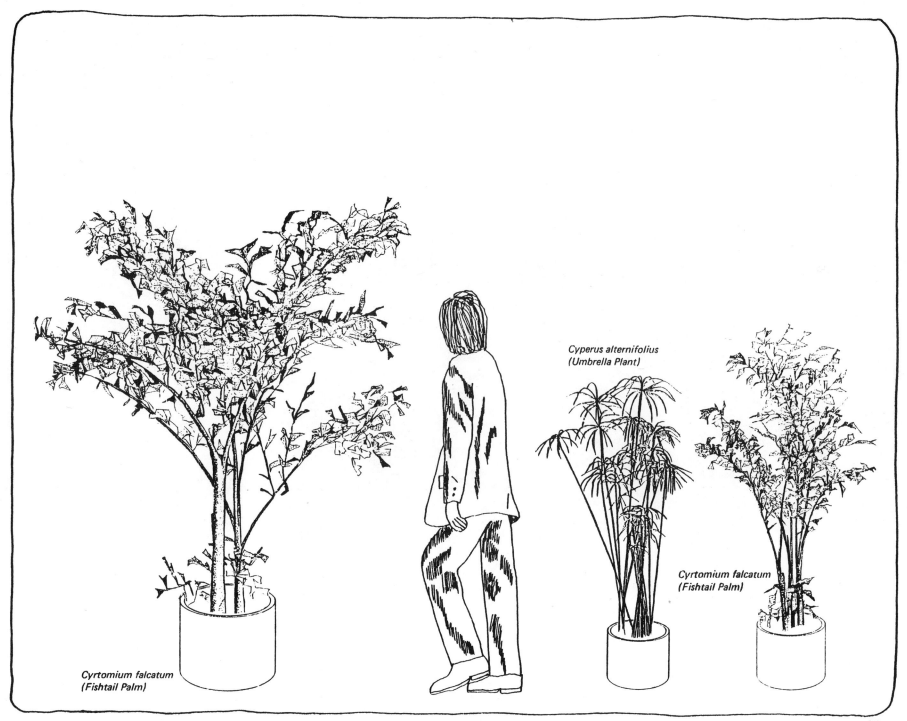

Cyrtomium falcatum
(Fishtail Palm)

Cyperus alternifolius
(Umbrella Plant)

Cyrtomium falcatum
(Fishtail Palm)

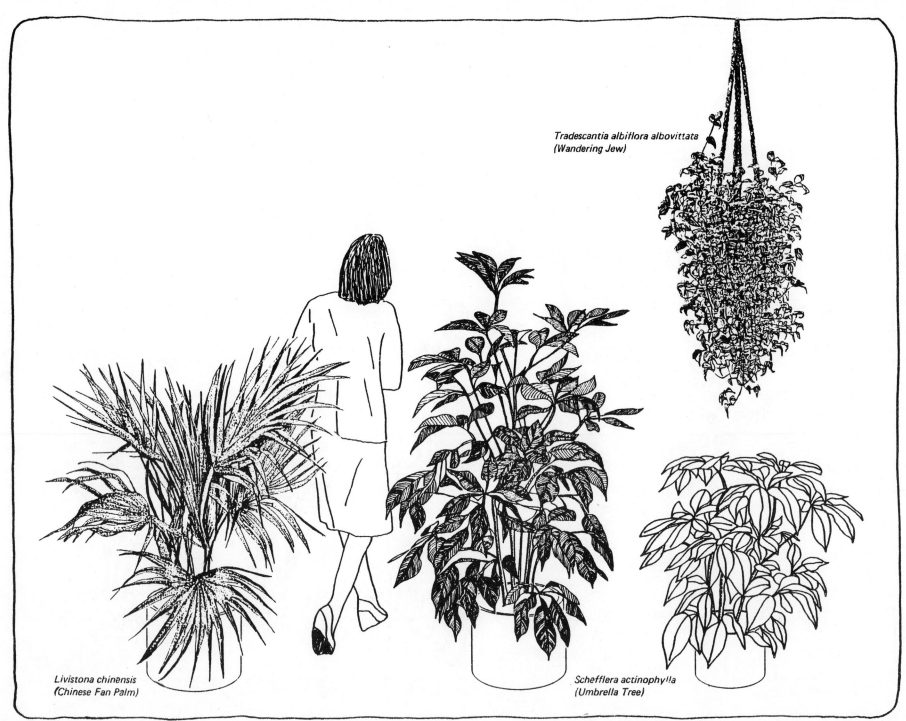

Tradescantia albiflora albovittata
(Wandering Jew)

Livistona chinensis
(Chinese Fan Palm)

Schefflera actinophylla
(Umbrella Tree)

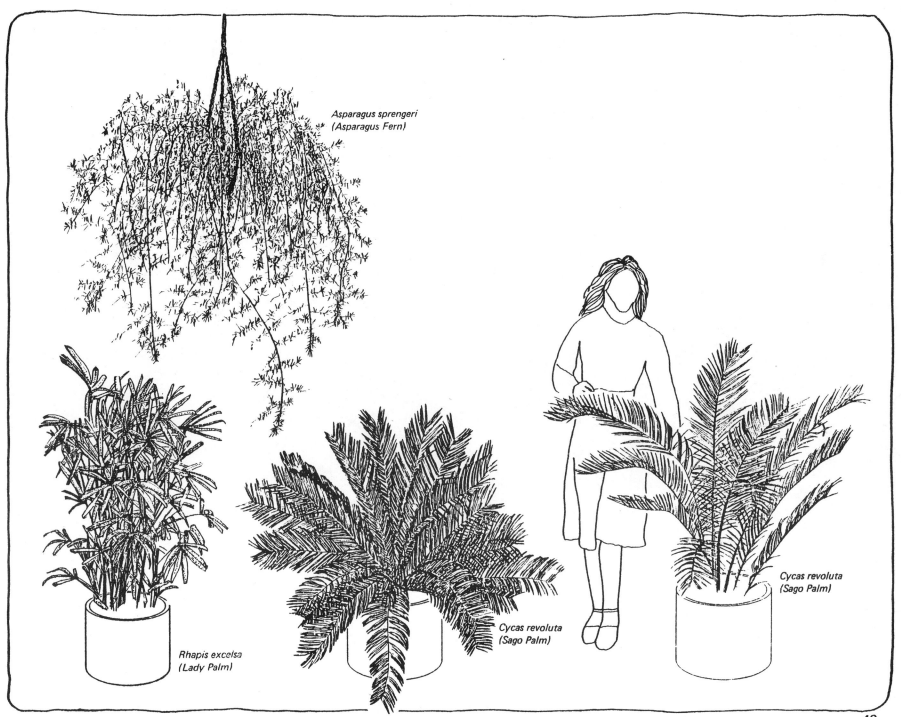

Asparagus sprengeri
(Asparagus Fern)

Rhapis excelsa
(Lady Palm)

Cycas revoluta
(Sago Palm)

Cycas revoluta
(Sago Palm)

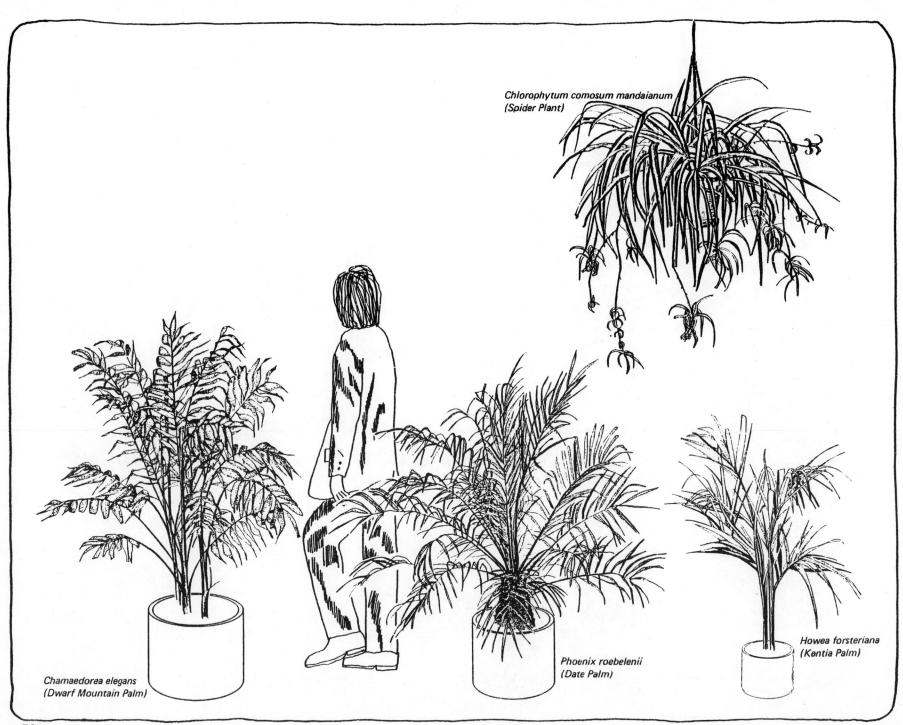

Chlorophytum comosum mandaianum
(Spider Plant)

Chamaedorea elegans
(Dwarf Mountain Palm)

Phoenix roebelenii
(Date Palm)

Howea forsteriana
(Kentia Palm)

Chamaerops humilis
(European Fan Palm)

Beaucarnea recurvata
(Pony Tail)

Dieffenbachia exotica
(Dumb Cane)

Dieffenbachia exotica
(Dumb Cane)

Aralia Balfouriana
(Balfour Aralia)

Cibotium schiedei
(Mexican Tree Fern)

52

Hedera helix
(English Ivy)

Dracaena deremensis 'Warneckei'
(Striped Dracaena)

Dracaena marginata
(Madagascar Dragon Tree)

Dracaena marginata
(Madagascar Dragon Tree)

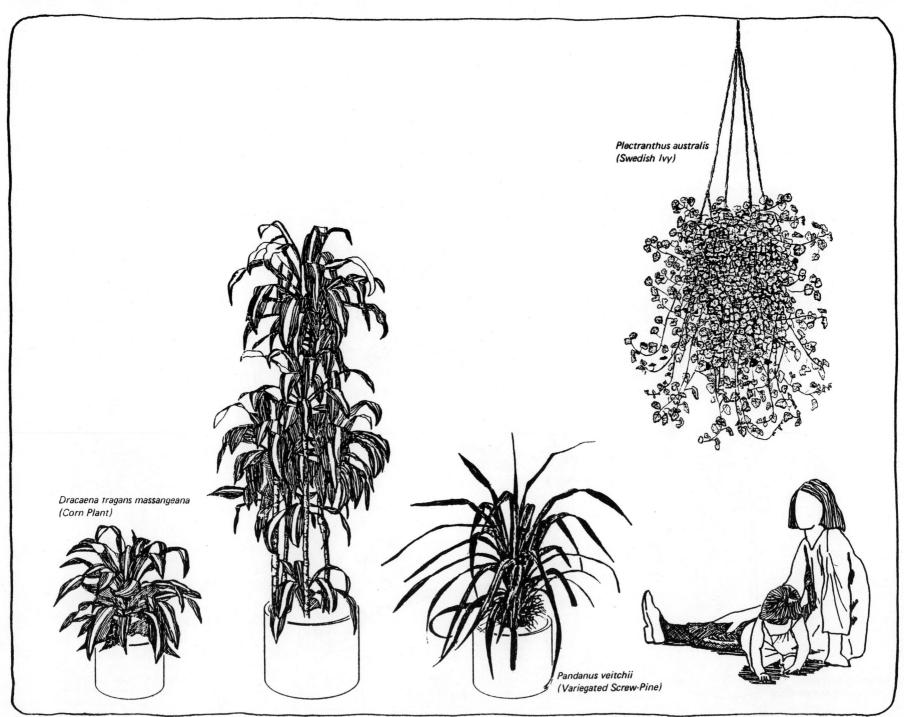

Plectranthus australis
(Swedish Ivy)

Dracaena tragans massangeana
(Corn Plant)

Pandanus veitchii
(Variegated Screw-Pine)

Pandanus veitchii
(Screw-Pine)

Pleomele relexa
(Maylasian Dracaena)

Dracaena deremensis 'Warneckei'
(Striped Dracaena)

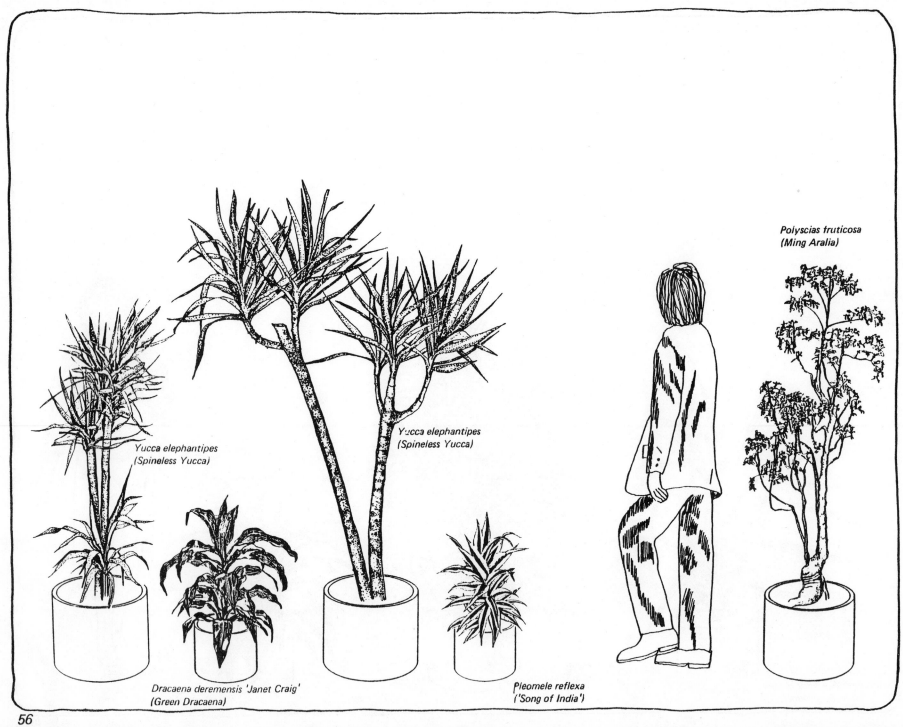

Yucca elephantipes
(Spineless Yucca)

Yucca elephantipes
(Spineless Yucca)

Polyscias fruticosa
(Ming Aralia)

Dracaena deremensis 'Janet Craig'
(Green Dracaena)

Pleomele reflexa
('Song of India')

56

Aechmea fasciata
(Bromeliad) **34, 57**

Ficus elastica
(Rubber Plant)

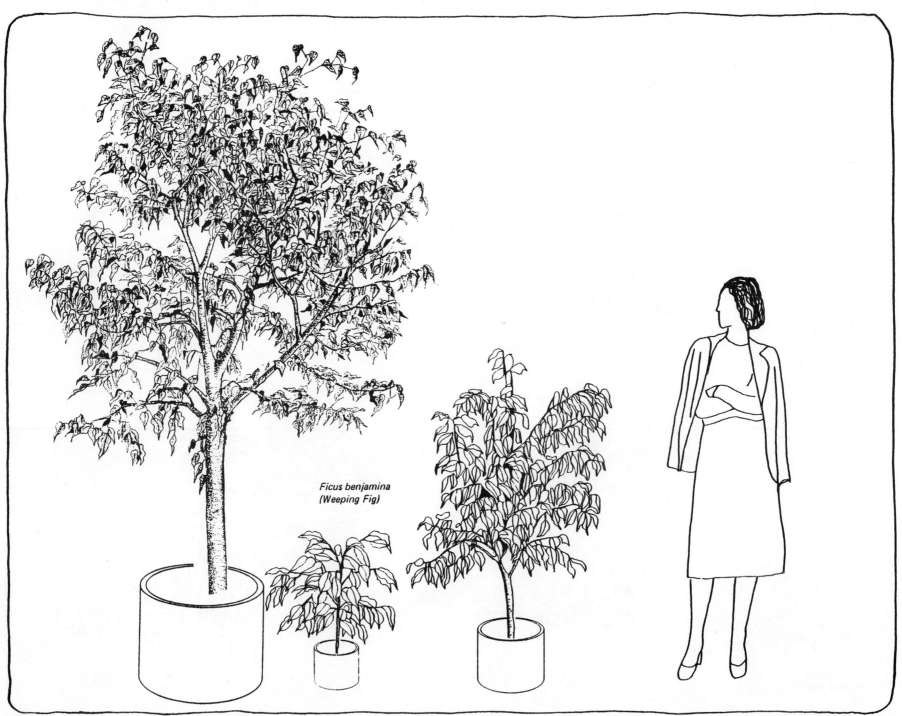

Ficus benjamina
(Weeping Fig)

58

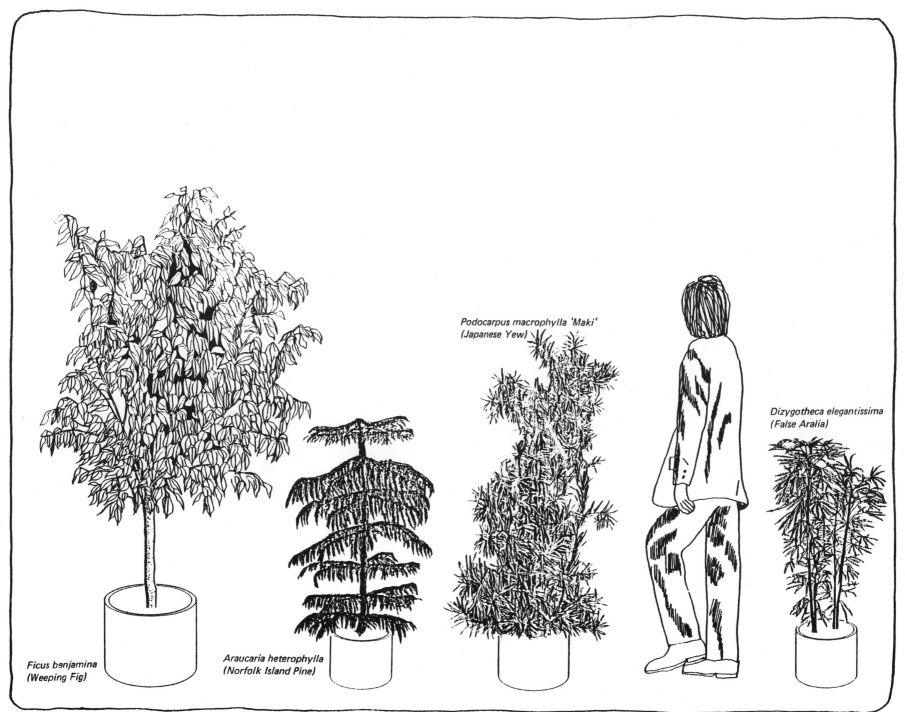

Podocarpus macrophylla 'Maki'
(Japanese Yew)

Dizygotheca elegantissima
(False Aralia)

Ficus benjamina
(Weeping Fig)

Araucaria heterophylla
(Norfolk Island Pine)

Dracaena deremensis 'Janet Craig'
(Green Dracaena)

Dracaena deremensis 'Warneckei'
(Striped Dracaena)

Dieffenbachia exotica
(Dumb Cane)

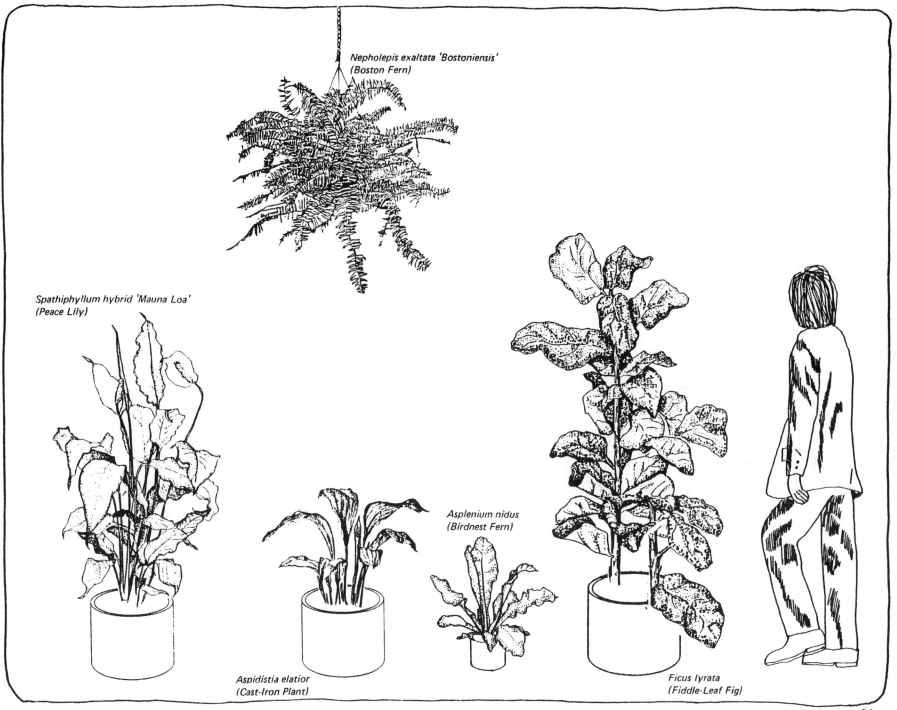

Nepholepis exaltata 'Bostoniensis'
(Boston Fern)

Spathiphyllum hybrid 'Mauna Loa'
(Peace Lily)

Aspidistia elatior
(Cast-Iron Plant)

Asplenium nidus
(Birdnest Fern)

Ficus lyrata
(Fiddle-Leaf Fig)

61

Ficus lyrata
(Fiddle-Leaf Fig)

Citrus mitis
(Calamondin Orange)

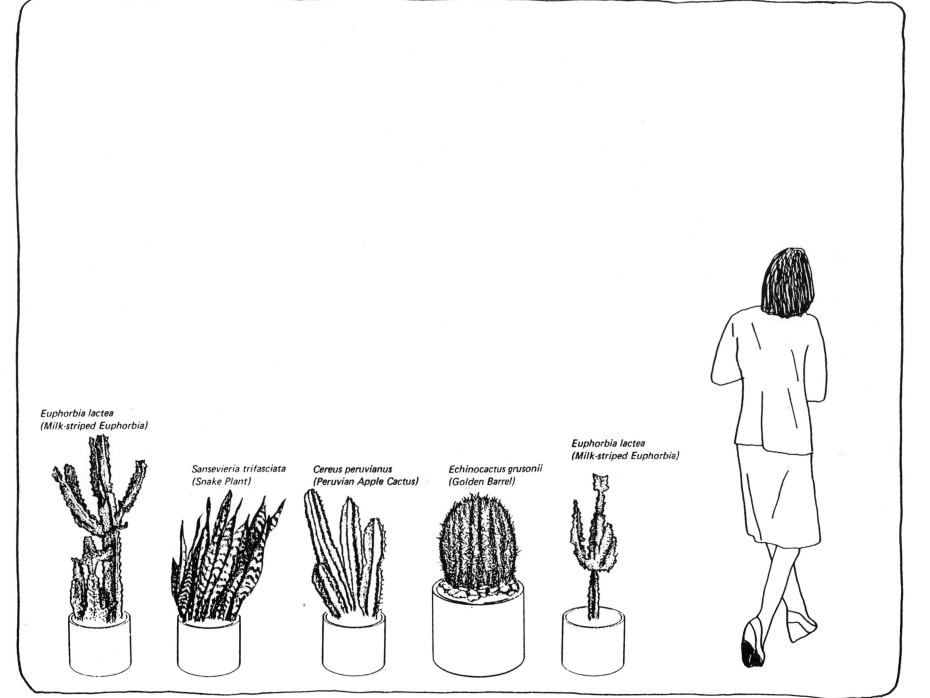

Euphorbia lactea
(Milk-striped Euphorbia)

Sansevieria trifasciata
(Snake Plant)

Cereus peruvianus
(Peruvian Apple Cactus)

Echinocactus grusonii
(Golden Barrel)

Euphorbia lactea
(Milk-striped Euphorbia)

INTERIOR
FOLIAGE PLANTS
GROUPINGS & ART

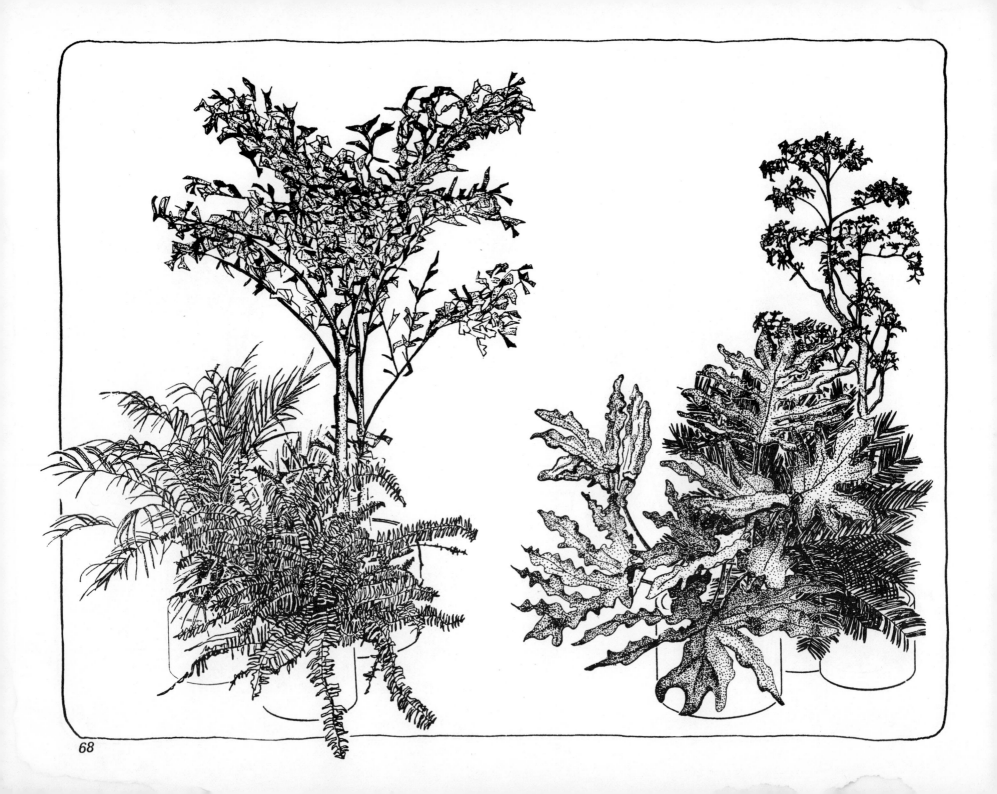

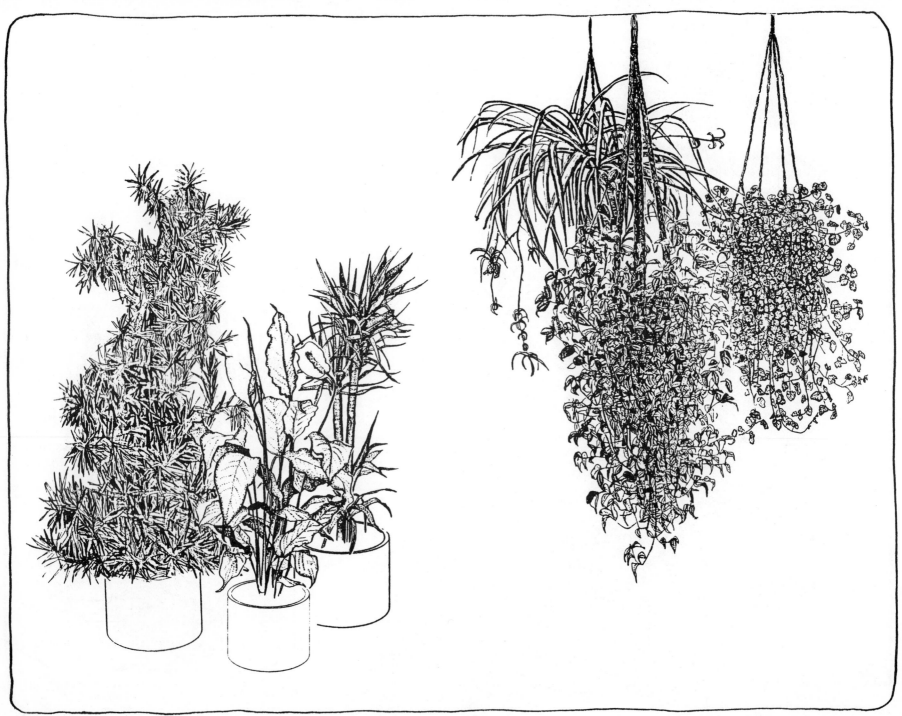

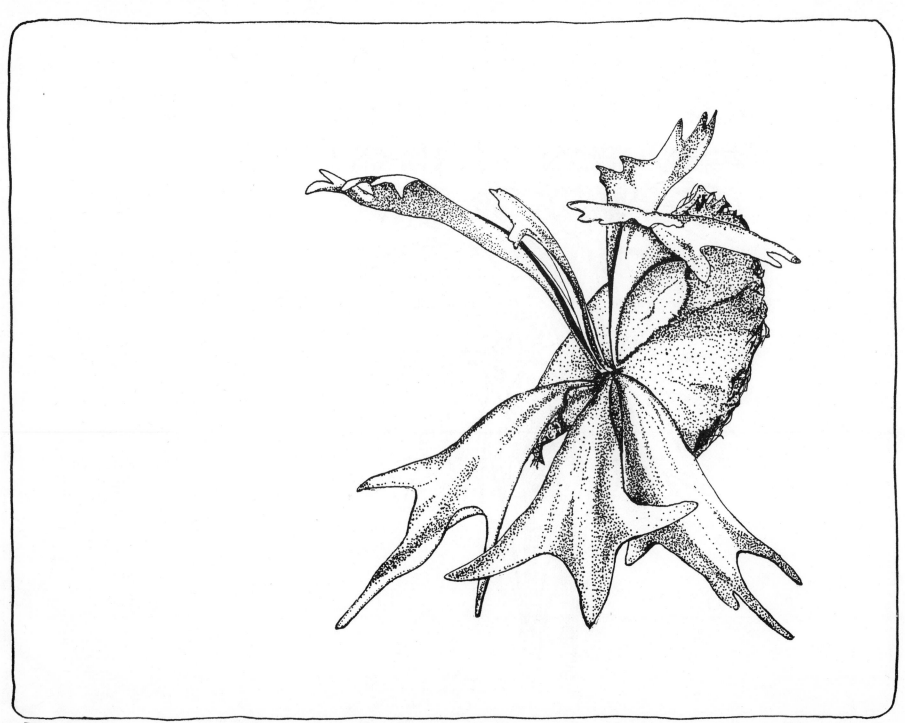

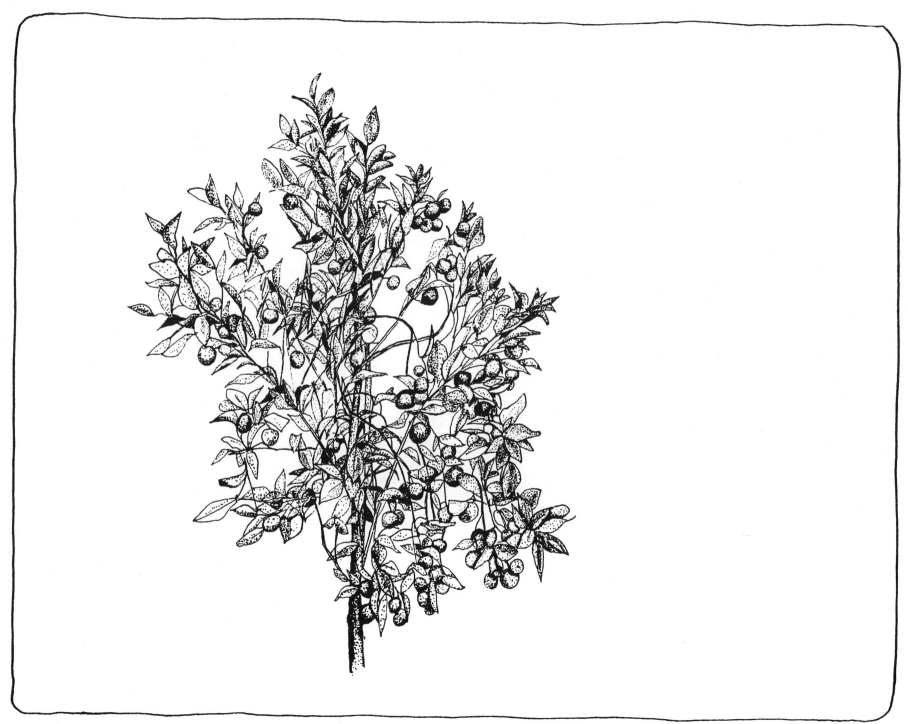

78